ALSO IN THE BLASTA BOOKS SERIES

Blasta Books #1: Tacos

Blasta Books #2: Hot Fat

Blasta Books #3: The United Nations
of Cookies

Blasta Books #4: Wok

Blasta Books #5: Soup

Blasta Books #6: Tapas

WASTED

Conor Spacey

CONTENTS

Introduction 1

Roasted carrots with carrot skin dukkah,
carrot top pesto & labneh 6

Pumpkin noodles with roasted pumpkin
seeds & pumpkin skin lardons 8

Salt-baked beetroot & leaf salad
with goat cheese & pickled beet stalks 10

It all starts with storage 12

Simple veg pickle 14

Piccalilli 15

Banana skin chutney 17

Five ways with stale bread 18

Sourdough panzanella with crispy egg,
chilli dressing & pickles 20

Ribollita 22

Seasoning & stock 23

Pasta with herb pesto, cheese fritters
& carrot skin crisps 24

Gnocchi with homemade ricotta 26

Whey hey hey bread 28

Five ways with whey 29

How to regrow food 30

Carrot & chilli Scotch eggs 32

Vegetable ramen 34

Five ways with broccoli stalks 37

Potato hash with broccomoli 38

How to make your own yogurt 39

Cauliflower bhajis with coriander yogurt
& flatbreads 40

All about aquafaba 42

Roast cabbage wedges with hummus,
peanuts & chilli oil 44

Five ways with fermentation 46

Fermentation top tips 51

Empty-the-fridge kimchi 52

Five ways with cheese 54

Cheesy kimchi toastie with Bloody Mary mayo 56

Sauerkraut fritters with poached eggs
& homemade yogurt 59

Pasta with mushrooms, kosho & toasted
Parmesan rind 60

Pineapple tepache margarita 61

Chocolate chip & coffee grounds cookies 62

Bread & jam pudding 63

Chester cake 64

Chocolate truffles 65

Index 66

INTRODUCTION

Hi. I'm Conor Spacey and I'm a waster.

The first step on a journey to eliminate food waste is to admit that you waste food. It can be overwhelming at times to get your head around the sheer amount of food loss and food waste across the globe. However, I'm a firm believer that if we all take little steps, then collectively we can make a big impact. You can also create fantastic dishes at home, which in turn will save you money, improve our broken food system and reduce climate change.

For me, this journey started many years ago. When I was 16, I moved to the UK with no idea what I wanted to do. Having sold my bass guitar, I had enough money in my pocket to keep me there for two weeks. With the clock ticking and no real work being offered to a young Irishman with no qualifications, I moved from job to job. I did a stint in a warehouse with a 5 a.m. start every day. I would climb a ladder with a hammer and chisel to remove lambs' hearts from a frozen wall and send them down a tube to get packaged at the other end. It paid my bills for a shitty shoebox bedsit with a two-ring electric stove, no oven, a counter fridge and a bathroom that was shared with 10 strangers. I stuck with it for a while but standing in a walk-in freezer all day chopping meat didn't really appeal to me.

From there, I was lured into the depths of a dark cellar kitchen that propped up a six-storey hotel to wash pots (I didn't really have a choice). That's where I began to witness food waste first-hand, from chefs piling up trays, pots and pans filled with leftovers or the ends of vegetables and fruits to the uneaten food on plates coming back from full diners. Working beside a bin, I would lose count of how many times I carried black sacks of perfectly good food from the wash-up area to the skips in the alleyway.

As a young guy who was just starting out in the world of commercial kitchens, I didn't have a voice. I couldn't express my feelings about seeing such waste, and to be honest, no one cared anyway. At this very early stage in my now long career, things like climate change, carbon footprints and sustainability weren't being discussed yet. All I knew was that this was wrong. Having grown up in a typical Irish household, we used everything. Nothing went to waste; that was the norm. I have fond memories of my dad growing food in the garden, mainly beans and potatoes. Seeing the hard work that went into growing food made you appreciate it and connected you to it.

My only choice was to work away and keep my mouth shut. Well, I wasn't very good at that. I remember it was Christmastime and hundreds of turkeys were being roasted every week in the hotel, the succulent meat carved into perfect slices, all in preparation of dinner celebrations. I took this opportunity to challenge the head chef. There I was, standing in his office in a pair of blue overalls. 'Well, Paddy, what do you want?' he barked.

'I've noticed how much turkey the chefs are cooking, and I've also noticed how much meat is left on the bones and being thrown away. If you let me break this meat down into ingredients that can be used for staff dinners, then can you teach me dishes to cook with it?'

'You want to learn how to cook, Paddy?' he laughed – the loudest laughter I've ever heard in my life, coming from a very small Scottish man. 'You're here to wash pots and walls and that's it.'

But I didn't give up. I was getting hooked on the atmosphere and adrenaline rush of the kitchen during a busy service and I wanted more. So off I went to his office again. 'What if I do this on my time, after my shift has finished? You'll have enough food to feed the team and I'll learn about cooking.' To my amazement, he agreed.

I stayed back every evening to go through all the production waste and segregate it into sections that could be repurposed into dishes the next day. In exchange, I was taught how to cook the basics: turkey curries, omelettes, frittatas, soups.

Then one day, an opportunity came my way. A trainee chef had become sick and was going to be out of action for a few weeks. I struck another deal: 'Let me work in your section, and if you're happy after three weeks, then promote me from pot-washer to trainee chef.'

'OK, Paddy,' he said, but this time he didn't laugh. It was as if he was starting to see that I really wanted to do this, that I, too, was a misfit who could easily fit into this family.

Over the years I moved around between different hotels, restaurants, pubs and bistros. I was like a sponge, soaking up everything and always learning. I focused on creating dishes with fantastic flavours, but I also focused on moving up the ranks, where I would then get a voice. I wanted to be able to make decisions on where our ingredients came from and ensure that I could create dishes that would use every part of every piece of food we bought.

I took my misfit status to a new level. What if I could be the misfit who questioned everything that we take for granted in the kitchen?

Today, my work has gone beyond the four walls of a professional kitchen. I'm involved in an organisation called the Chefs' Manifesto that covers over 100 countries, where we do a deep dive into the entire global food system and align our work with the UN Sustainable Development Goals. This not only gives us the tools to share our work with each other but also gives chefs a voice at the table to address the many issues in our food system.

ABOUT THIS BOOK

This book is vegetarian for two reasons. First, most of our household food waste comes from vegetables, breads and fruits. And second, I became a vegetarian almost five years ago. Why, I hear you ask. Part of my day-to-day job as a chef is to develop new dishes and ideas. I wanted to create more vegetarian dishes on our menus and felt that I needed to develop my tastebuds more so that I could come up with ideas for vegetable-focused dishes that tasted great. I set myself the challenge of giving up meat and fish for six months and never looked back. But I know that a vegetarian diet isn't for everyone, and that's okay. You could add meat, fish or poultry to many of the dishes in this book if you like, but you might be surprised how good the flavours and textures of the dishes are without meat.

While my experience is in professional kitchens, this book is focused on the food we cook at home and the staggering amount that we throw away. It contains just a handful of the many ideas, flavours and ways to use up surplus food that I've been working on for years now, because waste is not, and should never be, an option.

CLOSING THE LOOP

A closed loop recipe is where you really start to think about everything: every ingredient, every vegetable, every part. It's what I like to refer to as vegetable butchery – breaking down ingredients into all their delicious parts.

The following three recipes are an example of how to identify every part and incorporate them into fantastic dishes. Throughout this book you'll also find that parts of one dish lead to another dish, as illustrated in the mind map at the start of the book.

ROASTED CARROTS WITH CARROT SKIN DUKKAH, CARROT TOP PESTO AND LABNEH

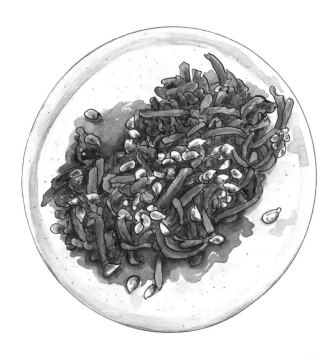

PUMPKIN NOODLES WITH ROASTED PUMPKIN SEEDS AND PUMPKIN SKIN LARDONS

SALT-BAKED BEETROOT AND LEAF SALAD WITH GOAT CHEESE AND PICKLED BEET STALKS

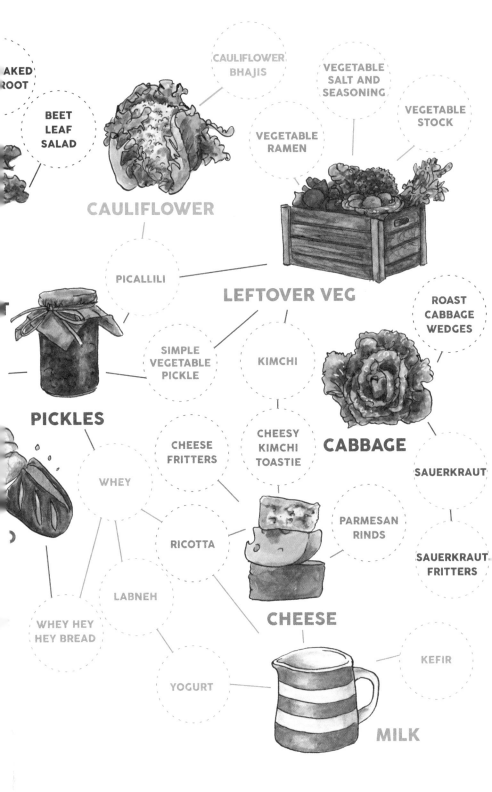

AKED ROOT

BEET LEAF SALAD

CAULIFLOWER BHAJIS

VEGETABLE SALT AND SEASONING

VEGETABLE STOCK

VEGETABLE RAMEN

CAULIFLOWER

PICALLILI

LEFTOVER VEG

ROAST CABBAGE WEDGES

PICKLES

SIMPLE VEGETABLE PICKLE

KIMCHI

CHEESE FRITTERS

CHEESY KIMCHI TOASTIE

CABBAGE

SAUERKRAUT

WHEY

RICOTTA

PARMESAN RINDS

SAUERKRAUT FRITTERS

LABNEH

CHEESE

WHEY HEY HEY BREAD

YOGURT

KEFIR

MILK

BANANA SKIN CHUTNEY

CULTURED VINEGAR

KOSHO

CHILLI OIL

SALT E BEET

PEELS & SKINS

CARROT SKIN CRISPS

CHILLI

CARROT & CHILLI SCOTCH EGGS

PUMPKIN SKIN LARDONS

CARROT SKIN DUKKAH

BEETROO

CARROT TOP PESTO

PICKLED BEET STALKS

PUMPKIN NOODLES

CARROT

ROASTED PUMPKIN SEEDS

PUMPKIN

ROAST CARROTS

RIBOLITTA

PANZANELLA

BREA

GNOCCHI

BREAD & JAM PUDDING

POTATO

POTATO HASH

CAKE

CHESTER CAKE

CHOCOLATE TRUFFLES

ROASTED CARROTS WITH CARROT SKIN DUKKAH, CARROT TOP PESTO & LABNEH

SERVES 2 AS A MAIN OR 4 AS A SIDE

I love to work with just one or two ingredients, and this dish is one of my favourites – so much so that it inspired the cover of this book. I like to think of vegetables the same way you would if it was piece of meat: butcher it into parts and ensure you use everything. This dish is a great example of that. More and more supermarkets are starting to sell bunches of whole carrots, including their tops. This gives you more for your money, as the tops are delicious in salads, pasta or turned into pesto. This dish works well as a light lunch or served family-style on a platter as a side for dinner.

1 bunch of carrots with the tops still on

a drizzle of rapeseed oil

fine sea salt and freshly ground black pepper

FOR THE CARROT SKIN DUKKAH:

50g nuts (use any nuts that you have – a great way to use up the ends of packets)

1 tbsp cumin seeds

1 tbsp coriander seeds

1 tbsp fennel seeds

1 tbsp sesame seeds

First, make the labneh. Stir the yogurt and salt together, then put a clean piece of cheesecloth or muslin into a strainer and set this over a bowl. Pour in the yogurt and tie the cloth into a knot. Put the bowl in the fridge for 24–48 hours, depending on how thick you like your labneh. I usually give it 48 hours so that it has a cheese-like consistency. Scrape the labneh out into an airtight container and store it in the fridge for up to three weeks. (Don't throw away the whey that has drained out of the yogurt! Use it to make the bread on page 28 or see page 29 for other ideas.)

To make the pesto, cut the tops off the bunch of carrots. Remove the thick stalks from the leafy carrot tops and chop them separately. Bring a pot of salted water to the boil. Have a bowl of iced water ready. Once the water is boiling, add the carrot tops and chopped stems and cook for 3 minutes, until bright green and tender. Drain, then immediately transfer the carrot tops and stems to the bowl of iced water to stop the cooking process and keep the vibrant colour.

Remove the carrot tops and stems from the cold water, squeeze out any excess liquid and spread them out on a chopping board to dry slightly.

FOR THE CARROT TOP PESTO:

4 spring onions

1 garlic clove, peeled and left whole

1 small bunch of fresh mint or basil, leaves picked

50g nuts (any kind)

½ lemon, zest and juice

3 tbsp rapeseed oil

FOR THE LABNEH:

400g natural yogurt (I love Velvet Cloud sheep milk yogurt)

¼ tsp fine sea salt

To make the pesto, put the spring onions, garlic, fresh herbs, nuts and the lemon zest and juice in a food processor and blend to a chunky paste. Add the rapeseed oil a little at a time until it's all combined. Season to taste with salt and pepper. Store the pesto in a sealed jar in the fridge for up to four weeks. It will separate slightly and naturally form a layer of oil on top, so just give it a stir before using.

To make the dukkah, preheat the oven to 140°C (120°C fan).

Peel the carrots, then spread out the skins on a baking tray (you should probably have around 20g of carrot skins). Cook in the preheated oven for 30 minutes, turning twice during the cooking time, until the skins are dried and crisp. Allow to cool completely – the skins will crisp up even more as they cool – then put the dried skins in a blender and blitz on a high speed until they're all finely chopped. Tip out into a bowl and set aside.

Increase the oven temperature to 200°C (180°C fan).

Mix the nuts and seeds together in a bowl, then spread them out on another baking tray and cook for 8–10 minutes, until nicely toasted. Allow to cool completely, then transfer to the blender and pulse two or three times – you want them to be chopped but not smooth.

Tip out into the bowl with the carrot skins and stir everything together with a wooden spoon. You can store the dukkah in a sealed container for up to four weeks at this point.

Increase the oven temperature again, this time to 210°C (190°C fan).

If you're using small or baby carrots, you can leave them whole. If you're using larger carrots, cut them at an angle so that they're the size of your finger. Put the carrots in a bowl, drizzle with rapeseed oil and season with salt and pepper. Toss to coat them well, then spread them out on a baking tray and roast in the oven for 15 minutes, until they start to colour and still have a slight bite.

To serve, roll the roasted carrots in some of the dukkah. Put them on a serving plate with a big spoonful of labneh on top, then drizzle over some of the pesto.

PUMPKIN NOODLES WITH ROASTED PUMPKIN SEEDS & PUMPKIN SKIN LARDONS

SERVES 4

Pumpkin is not just for Halloween! Their season usually starts in September and continues into early December. We waste so many perfectly edible pumpkins for the Halloween holiday to decorate our homes and never eat them. This recipe uses the entire pumpkin. You can also use butternut squash if you can't get your hands on a pumpkin.

1 small or medium pumpkin or 1 butternut squash

a pinch of chilli powder

a pinch of paprika

fine sea salt and freshly ground black pepper

40g butter

rapeseed oil

100g baby spinach

Preheat the oven to 200°C (180°C fan).

Cut the pumpkin into wedges so that it's easier to manage. Aim for six wedges for a medium pumpkin or four wedges for a small one or a butternut squash. Using a spoon, scoop out all the seeds and any loose bits of flesh from the centre of each wedge and set aside. Using a sturdy vegetable peeler or a sharp knife, carefully remove the skin from each piece and set it aside.

If you're into kitchen gadgets, then this is the time to get your spiralizer out of the cupboard and turn that pumpkin flesh into pumpkin spaghetti. Or you can just use a sharp knife to cut the wedges lengthways into long, thin strips.

To make the pumpkin skin lardons, cut the skins into small squares, like bacon lardons. Put them in a bowl and season with the chilli powder, paprika, salt and pepper, then spread them out on a baking tray. Roast in the preheated oven for 20 minutes, stirring them around halfway through, until they are crisp.

Increase the oven temperature to 210°C (190°C fan).

Meanwhile, blanch the pumpkin seeds – it's the easiest way to remove the pieces of pumpkin flesh clinging to them. Bring a pot of water to the boil, add the seeds and boil for 1 minute, then drain and cool under cold running water. Rub the seeds between your fingers to remove any flesh, then spread them out on a baking tray and put a clean

tea towel over them to soak up any excess water. Drizzle over some rapeseed oil and sprinkle with paprika and salt, tossing so that the seeds are all evenly coated. Roast in the oven for 20 minutes, then set aside to cool.

Now it's time to bring it all together. Melt the butter with a splash of rapeseed oil in a large non-stick frying pan. Add the pumpkin noodles, season with salt and cook, stirring, for 2 minutes, until warmed through – you're not really cooking these, just warming them up and softening them a little. Add the pumpkin skin lardons and baby spinach and cook just until the spinach has wilted slightly.

To serve, divide the noodles, lardons and spinach between four plates and top with the pumpkin seeds.

SALT-BAKED BEETROOT & LEAF SALAD WITH GOAT CHEESE & PICKLED BEET STALKS

SERVES 4

Beetroot and goat cheese? Yes, please! This classic combination uses the entire beetroot to introduce new flavours that will wake up even the most dormant taste-buds. Baking the beetroots in a salt crust intensifies their flavour and is well worth trying – it's my favourite recipe in the book.

4 medium beetroots (heritage varieties in different colours are great if you can get them)

500g plain flour

150g fine sea salt

2 egg whites

200ml cold water

150g soft goat cheese

a drizzle of rapeseed oil

40g roasted nuts, roughly chopped

Begin by breaking down the beetroots into three parts: roots, stalks and leaves.

You need to start this dish the day before you want to serve it to give the beetroot stalks time to pickle. I normally cut the stalks in half (though this depends on the size of your jar) and pickle them using the recipe on page 14. Leave them for at least one day but you could let them pickle for months.

The leaves need to be washed, gently dried with a clean tea towel, then wrapped in damp kitchen paper and stored in the fridge.

To make the salt crust, put the flour, salt and egg whites in a blender and blitz until well combined, then add the cold water and blend again to form a dough. Tip the dough out onto a clean countertop and knead until you form a smooth ball. Put the dough in a bowl, cover it with a clean cloth and chill in the fridge for 1 hour.

Preheat the oven to 190°C (170°C fan).

Roll the dough out until it's about 1cm thick, then divide it into four even pieces. Put a beetroot in the centre of each piece, then press the sides of the dough around each beetroot until it's totally covered. Put the salt-crusted beetroots on a baking tray and cook in the preheated oven for 2½ hours.

Remove the tray from the oven. When the beetroots are cool enough to handle, break off the crust – the beetroot skins will peel away very easily just using your hands.

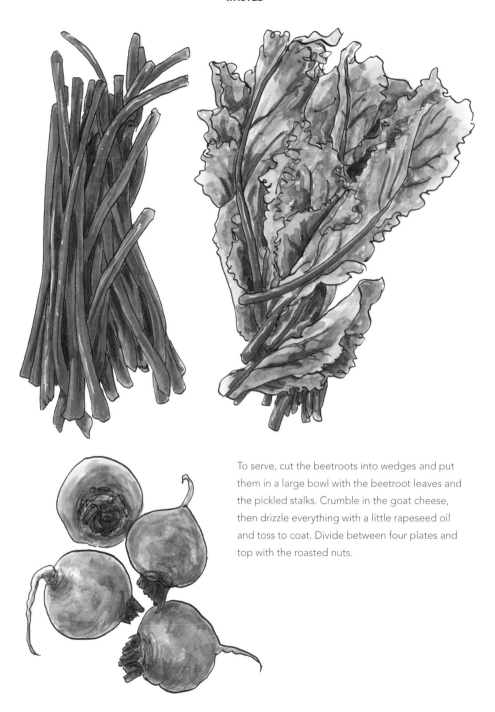

To serve, cut the beetroots into wedges and put them in a large bowl with the beetroot leaves and the pickled stalks. Crumble in the goat cheese, then drizzle everything with a little rapeseed oil and toss to coat. Divide between four plates and top with the roasted nuts.

IT ALL STARTS WITH STORAGE

How you store your food can lead to waste before you even get a chance to eat or cook with the ingredients you've bought.

ROOT VEG

A lot of people return home with their shopping and put everything in the fridge, but root vegetables (potatoes, carrots, onions, etc.) are best left out of the fridge. If you have the space, it's worth buying a small rack that will fit in a cupboard and store your root veg there. Make sure you remove any plastic packaging on the veg, as this will make them 'sweat' and go off quicker.

FRUIT

If the fruit you buy is underripe (which it usually is in most supermarkets), then it's best to keep it in a fruit bowl at room temperature. This helps the fruit to ripen and makes it better to eat. When the fruit is ripe but you know you won't eat it all in the next few days, then it's time to put it in the fridge to slow down the ripening process and to keep it at its best for longer. Bananas, however, will ripen quicker in a fridge and are best left at room temperature until eaten. If you eat whole fruits like melons, pineapples, etc., leave them out of the fridge until you cut them, then keep in your fridge after that.

SIBLING RIVALRY

Some fruit and vegetables just don't get on together. A bit like that certain sibling or cousin at a family gathering, they need to be kept separated. Without getting too scientific, fruits and vegetables release a type of gas (which is totally harmless to us). Some produce more gas than others, which can affect the ripening process of other fruit and veg that are stored near them. When it comes to fruit, the biggest culprits are apples, bananas, peaches and plums – these bad boys need to be stored in their own bowl and kept away from broccoli, cauliflower, kale, leeks, mushrooms and potatoes. The gas that these fruits give off is like kryptonite to these vegetables.

FRESH HERBS

If you're fond of using fresh herbs in your cooking (and why wouldn't you be?), then buy them in pots from your shop or supermarket. This way, you can keep them in your kitchen (on your windowsill or counter), water them regularly and take only what you need, when you need it, and they will continue to grow.

If you don't use fresh herbs that often, though, then remove them from their packaging, wash them in a salad spinner, wrap them in damp kitchen paper and store them in the fridge. This will keep them fresher for longer.

SIMPLE VEG PICKLE

MAKES 1 LARGE JAR

I've spent years researching food and how our attitudes towards ingredients and even meals have changed over the generations. One thing that always strikes me is that a lot of the solutions to food waste can be found in the past.

Pickling food to preserve it for the winter months when nothing is growing is an ancient (and delicious) method that goes back thousands of years. It's a great way to use surplus ingredients that you may have in your fridge or cupboard. Many of us have the habit of buying more than we need. You know how it goes: you're making a dish that needs one red onion, so you buy six of them in a net. The other five are left to one side with good intentions to use them in another dish, but it doesn't happen.

Well, here is my go-to, simple pickling recipe for those situations. It works with pretty much any vegetable – believe me, I've tried them all.

225g vegetables (you can use any vegetable)

2 red onions

500ml apple cider vinegar

150g caster sugar

30g fine sea salt

15g chilli flakes

10g whole mustard seeds

Wash your vegetables, pat them dry and slice or cut into small pieces. Peel your onions, cut them in half, then thinly slice.

Put the vinegar, sugar, salt, chilli flakes and mustard seeds in a saucepan and bring to a boil, then remove the pan from the heat and let it cool.

Put the veg and onions in a large sterilised Kilner jar (see page 51 for instructions on how to sterilise the jar), then pour in the cooled pickling brine. Close the lid and give the jar a shake.

Leave the jar out on your kitchen counter or in a cool, dry cupboard for three weeks, then refrigerate to stop the fermentation. These pickles will keep for up to six months.

PICCALILLI

MAKES 1 x 500ML JAR

You can buy perfectly good piccalilli from the shops, but for me it's yet another way to repurpose any half-used vegetables I've got lying around. I love it with my carrot and chilli Scotch eggs (page 32) but it's also good with cheese, cold meats and salads.

150g cauliflower (use it all – florets, leaves and stalks)

60g root vegetables such as carrots and/or celery, cut into small chunks

60g onion, chopped

30g green vegetables, such as courgettes, beans and/or mangetout, cut into small pieces

2 tbsp fine sea salt

1 tbsp plain flour

1 tbsp English mustard powder

1 tbsp mustard seeds

½ tbsp coriander seeds

1 tsp cumin seeds

1 tsp ground turmeric

200ml white wine vinegar (or see the tip)

70g caster sugar

TRY THIS

Instead of using white wine vinegar, you could use your own cultured vinegar if you've made it from fruit scraps – see page 46.

Break the head of cauliflower into small florets. Keep the small leaves whole and chop the stalks and big leaves into small pieces. Put the florets, leaves and stalks in a large bowl with the rest of the vegetables. Add 1 tablespoon of the salt and mix it through gently with your hands, then leave out at room temperature for 1–2 hours. Wash the vegetables under cold running water and make sure you drain them well.

Put the flour, mustard powder, seeds and turmeric in a small bowl. Add 20ml of the vinegar and mix to form a paste.

Put the rest of the vinegar in a large pot with the sugar and the remaining tablespoon of salt. Slowly heat until the sugar and salt have dissolved, then add the mustard spice paste. Continue to cook on a low heat, stirring occasionally, until the mixture thickens. Stir in the drained veg and continue to cook for 1 more minute, then remove from the heat and immediately spoon into a sterilised 500ml jar (see page 51 for instructions on how to sterilise the jar).

Seal the jar with the lid and leave in a dark cupboard for at least five weeks, or up to three months for a stronger flavour. Once open, keep the piccalilli in the fridge and use it within six weeks.

BANANA SKIN CHUTNEY

MAKES 1 x 500ML JAR

Chutneys are so easy to make and so versatile – think of them as a savoury jam. They are fantastic served with cheese, cold and cured meats, grilled vegetables, in sandwiches or even added to a sauce or gravy for extra depth of flavour.

A banana skin chutney may sound strange, but trust me, it works. Years ago I met a chef from Brazil who told me a story about how he and other chefs used surplus foods from the Olympic Village at the Rio Olympics to feed people who didn't have access to a hot meal. One day they had planned on making a pasta dish with the understanding that they were also going to get ham. Well, that didn't happen, but in a stroke of genius they were able to substitute the ham with banana skins from the bananas that they did get. He also told me about the banana skin chutney he made, so I tweaked his recipe to come up with my own version.

1 tbsp vegetable or rapeseed oil

250g diced onion

2 fresh red or green chillies, chopped

2 tbsp ground turmeric

1 tbsp mustard seeds

1 tsp coriander seeds

2 green cardamom pods

6 over-ripe bananas, skins finely diced

1 regular banana, skins finely diced and fruit chopped

1 tbsp light brown sugar

a pinch of salt

4 whole cloves

2 star anise

1 cinnamon stick

500ml orange juice, plus extra if needed

Heat the oil in a pot set over a medium heat. Add the onion, chillies, turmeric, mustard and coriander seeds and cardamom pods. Cook, stirring occasionally, for about 5 minutes, until soft. Add the chopped banana skins, chopped banana, brown sugar and a pinch of salt. Wrap up the cloves, star anise and cinnamon stick in a small clean cloth and tie it with string (this makes it easier to remove them at the end), then add this to the pot. Pour in the orange juice, reduce the heat to low and cook for 10 minutes, stirring occasionally, until the skins have softened down to a jam-like consistency.

Remove and discard the cloth with the spices, then blend the chutney with a hand blender until semi-smooth. If it's too thick, add a little more orange juice or water until you get the right consistency.

Allow to cool completely, then transfer the chutney to a sterilised jar (see page 51) and keep it in your fridge for up to two months.

STALE BREAD

Bread is the most wasted food item in our homes. We often buy a full loaf even if we know we'll never eat it all, plus bread has a very short shelf life. Use stale bread in recipes like panzanella (page 20) or ribollita (page 22) or try these easy ideas.

1 BREADCRUMBS
Tear the bread into chunks, put it in a food processer or blender and blitz into crumbs. Keep in freezerproof bags in the freezer and take out what you need.

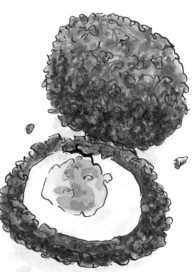

2 CROUTONS
Preheat your oven to 200°C (180°C fan). Cut your bread into 2.5cm squares. Spread it out on a baking tray, drizzle with rapeseed oil, sprinkle with flaky sea salt and bake in the hot oven for 10 minutes, until golden and crisp.

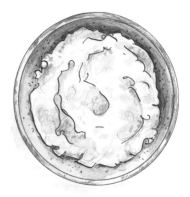

3 BREAD HUMMUS

You can use stale bread to make a hummus-type dip. Tear your bread into 2.5cm chunks, then put it in a food processor or blender and blitz into crumbs. Add 3 sliced garlic cloves and 2 tablespoons tahini and blend again. With the motor running, slowly add 120ml rapeseed oil, 4 tablespoons white wine vinegar and just enough water (or aquafaba – see page 42) to get it to come together into a smooth paste. Season with salt.

4 EGGY BREAD (AKA FRENCH TOAST)

The golden rule is to allow one egg per person per thick slice. Using that ratio, beat one whole egg with a pinch of ground cinnamon in a wide, shallow bowl. Dip a slice of bread into the beaten egg, turning to coat both sides. Let it sit for a minute to soak up all up the egg. Heat a splash of oil and a knob of butter in a non-stick frying pan over a medium heat. Add the bread to the hot pan and cook on both sides until golden. Serve with maple syrup poured over the top and fresh fruit.

5 GARLIC BREAD

Mix together 100g softened butter, 2 crushed garlic cloves, 2 teaspoons chopped fresh parsley and a pinch of flaky sea salt. Put slices of stale bread on a baking tray and spread copious amounts of the garlic butter on top. Put the tray under a hot grill for 2–3 minutes, until the bread is toasted and the butter has melted. Sprinkle a little of your favourite grated cheese on top of the slices if you like and pop back under the grill again until it's melted.

SOURDOUGH PANZANELLA WITH CRISPY EGG, CHILLI DRESSING & PICKLES

SERVES 4

Panzanella is an Italian salad that is traditionally made with stale bread tossed with onions, tomatoes, vinegar and olive oil. I add my homemade pickles and chilli oil for a little kick, tear some fresh mozzarella or burrata into it and top it with a crispy fried egg for the ultimate lunch. It's summer on a plate, using the food that is most often wasted at home: bread.

200g (or ½ loaf) stale sourdough bread

2 tbsp rapeseed oil, plus extra for frying

coarse sea salt and freshly ground black pepper

500g tomatoes, cut into quarters (use different varieties if you can)

100g pickled vegetables (page 14)

6 tbsp chilli oil (page 44 or shop-bought)

3 tbsp red wine vinegar

2 balls of fresh mozzarella or burrata

4 eggs

a handful of fresh basil

Preheat the oven to 200°C (180°C fan).

Tear or cut the sourdough into 3cm cubes and spread them out on a baking tray. Drizzle with the rapeseed oil and season with a pinch of coarse sea salt, then bake in the preheated oven for 10 minutes, until the bread is golden.

Put the cut tomatoes in a bowl, season with salt and leave for 5 minutes. Remove the pickled vegetables from the jar, making sure they are well drained of any brine, then add them to the tomatoes. Add the toasted bread and gently mix everything together with your hands, then add the chilli oil and red wine vinegar and season again with a pinch of salt and some pepper. Tear or shred the mozzarella or burrata into large pieces and add to the bowl, gently tossing it all together.

To fry the eggs, heat a splash of rapeseed oil in a non-stick frying pan over a medium heat. Crack your eggs into the pan one at a time and fry for 2 minutes. Season with salt and pepper. If you like your eggs more well done, then gently turn them over to cook on both sides.

To serve, divide the salad between four plates or put it all on one large serving platter. Top with the crispy fried eggs and tear over the basil leaves.

RIBOLLITA

SERVES 4–6

This Italian classic comes from Tuscany. The word 'ribollita' means 'to reboil', which is an important part of the process for extra flavour. This is best made a day in advance using surplus vegetables and stale bread, then reheated and enjoyed on a cold day (though pretty much any day will do), but it can of course be eaten straightaway if you can't resist. Traditionally this soup is based on root veg and kale, while onion, carrot and celery are typically used for the base, but I swap out the vegetables for whatever needs to be used up at the end of the week.

rapeseed oil, for cooking and drizzling

2 garlic cloves, chopped

1 tsp chilli flakes

1 tsp fennel seeds

1 onion, chopped into 1cm dice

1 carrot, chopped into 1cm dice

2 celery stalks, chopped into 1cm dice

a few sprigs of fresh thyme or rosemary, leaves or needles stripped from the stalks

fine sea salt and freshly ground black pepper

1 x 400g tin of whole plum tomatoes

1 x 400g tin of cannellini beans (or any tinned beans you want to use up)

1.5 litres vegetable stock or water

outer leaves of cabbage or 2 handfuls of kale or any leafy greens, chopped

½ loaf of stale bread, torn into small chunks

Heat a splash of rapeseed oil in a large pot set on a medium heat. Add the garlic, chilli flakes and fennel seeds and cook for 2 minutes. Add the onion, carrot and celery (or whichever vegetables you're using) and the thyme or rosemary, then season with salt and pepper. Reduce the heat to low and cook for 15 minutes, stirring occasionally. You want the vegetables to soften and caramelise slightly for extra flavour.

Add the tinned tomatoes, tinned beans (including their liquid) and the stock or water. Bring to the boil, then reduce the heat and simmer for 20 minutes, until the veg are all cooked and the liquid is starting to thicken. Add the cabbage, kale or greens to the soup and cook for another 10 minutes. (If you're making this soup in advance, I would stop at this stage, then reheat it and add the bread when you're ready to serve.)

Add the bread to the soup and simmer gently until the bread has broken down and the soup is thick and creamy. Season with salt and pepper, then ladle into bowls and drizzle some rapeseed oil on top.

SEASONING & STOCK

VEGETABLE & SALT SEASONING

This is a neat trick for using up vegetable skins to season the vegetables you're cooking. We tend to think that we always need to peel vegetables (and in some cases we do), but if you're using young, in-season root vegetables, it's not always necessary. I usually give them a good scrub in cold water and then use them as is. However, there are times when using bigger root vegetables (and of course onions) that you do need to peel them, but you can use the skins to add flavour to your food.

Preheat your oven to 140°C (120°C fan). Simply put your vegetable skins on a baking tray, spread them out evenly in a single layer and sprinkle with sea salt. Cook them in the preheated oven for 20–30 minutes, until they have completely dried out. Put the dried skins in a high-powered blender, such as a NutriBullet, and pulse into a powder. Mix the powder with an equal amount of good sea salt to create a 50/50 mix. Use it to season vegetables, sauces and soups.

VEGETABLE STOCK

You can freeze all your odds and ends of raw vegetables until you have enough to make this. However, it's best not to use artichokes, broccoli, Brussels sprouts, cabbage, cauliflower, swedes and turnips as their strong flavours can be too overpowering.

Here I'm using the most common vegetables that you may have at home, but you can use whatever you have: 4 leeks, tops and ends; 2 carrots, skins on; 1 onion, skin on; ½ head or root of celery; 4 garlic cloves, skin on and smashed; stalks and ends from fresh herbs like rosemary, parsley and/or thyme; and 6 whole black peppercorns. Cut all the veg into similar-sized chunks. Put them in a large pot with the garlic, herbs, peppercorns and a pinch of salt, then pour in 2 litres of water. Bring to the boil on a high heat, then reduce to a simmer and cook, uncovered, for 2 hours, until reduced slightly. Pass through a sieve and discard all the solids. The stock will keep for up to two weeks in the fridge or up to three months in the freezer. Use it for soups, sauces or as the perfect base for the vegetable ramen on page 34.

PASTA WITH HERB PESTO, CHEESE FRITTERS & CARROT SKIN CRISPS

SERVES 4

It's nearly the end of the week and you're staring into your fridge and cupboard, wondering what you can do with some leftover herbs, stale bread, odds and ends of different cheeses, a few dodgy carrots and a bag of pasta. Well hey presto, this dish will come to your rescue. But it's so good that you won't want to save it just for those times when the cupboards are bare.

400g of your favourite pasta (I love spaghetti or tagliatelle here or use leftover cooked pasta – see the tips)

180ml herb pesto (or see the tip)

FOR THE CHEESE FRITTERS:

500ml full-fat milk

80g plain flour, plus extra for dredging

60g butter, diced

150g cheese (any kind), grated or chopped into small pieces

4 dashes of Worcestershire sauce (or soy sauce to keep it vegetarian)

fine sea salt and freshly ground black pepper

2 egg yolks

1 whole egg, beaten

200g breadcrumbs

rapeseed or sunflower oil, for deep-frying

FOR THE CARROT SKIN CRISPS:

4 carrots, peels only

To make the fritters, pour the milk into a pot set over a medium heat and slowly heat but do not allow it to boil. When it starts to foam on top, whisk in the flour and butter and cook for 3 minutes, until it is thickened, smooth and silky and the flour has been cooked out. Reduce the heat slightly and add the cheese and the Worcestershire or soy sauce, stirring with a wooden spoon until the cheese has completely melted. Season with salt and pepper, then remove the pot from the heat and allow to cool slightly before whisking in the egg yolks. Pour into a baking tray that's at least 2.5cm deep and put in the fridge for at least 2 hours, until set firm.

Meanwhile, preheat the oven to 140°C (120°C fan).

To make the carrot skin crisps while the fritters are chilling, spread out your carrot skins on a baking tray, season with salt and cook in the preheated oven for 30 minutes, turning twice during the cooking time, until the skins are dried and crisp. Remove from the oven and allow to cool completely – the skins will crisp up even more as they cool.

Now back to the fritters. Heat the oil in a deep-fryer to 180°C (or see the tip on page 33). Line a baking tray with kitchen paper and set a wire rack on top of it.

Cut the cheese fritter mixture into 12 pieces, each about 5cm square. Get three wide, shallow bowls. Put some plain flour in the first bowl, the beaten egg in the second and the breadcrumbs in the third. Working with one at a time, first coat each fritter in the flour, then dip into the beaten

24

egg, ensuring that it is totally covered before shaking off any excess. Finally, dredge it in the breadcrumbs.

Carefully add four to six fritters to the hot oil (you need to cook them in batches so that you don't overcrowd the fryer or the pot). Fry for 2 minutes, then turn them over with a wooden spoon and cook for 1 minute more, until golden. Use a slotted spoon to transfer the fritters to the wire rack on top of the lined tray to drain off any excess oil. Keep warm.

Bring a pot of salted water to the boil. Add the pasta and cook according to the packet instructions (I always cook pasta for 3 minutes less than what it says on the packet so that it's still al dente). Or if you're using leftover pasta, cook it in the boiling salted water for just 2 minutes to reheat it. Drain and put the pasta back into the pot set over a low heat, then stir in the pesto and heat slightly until warm.

To serve, divide the pasta between four bowls. Put three fritters on top of each portion, then top with the carrot skin crisps.

TOP TIPS

I always cook more pasta or noodles than I need for one recipe. That way, I have some cooked in the fridge, ready to go, so that I can put together another meal in minutes, like the surplus vegetable ramen on page 34. When storing cooked pasta, allow it to cool, then use your hands to rub some rapeseed oil through it to prevent it from sticking together. Keep it in a sealed airtight container (like a lunch box) in the fridge for up to four days.

The carrot top pesto on page 6 works great here or you can follow the same recipe but replace the carrot tops with fresh herbs.

GNOCCHI WITH HOMEMADE RICOTTA

SERVES 4

Gnocchi date back centuries in Italian cuisine and there are many regional variations. These little pillows are delicious with your favourite herbs and cheese and are a great way to use up leftover mashed potatoes and surplus milk. It's an inexpensive meal to prepare and gnocchi lend themselves to pretty much any type of sauce and flavour.

500g leftover mashed potatoes (4 medium potatoes if making from scratch)

1 small egg, lightly beaten

100g plain flour, plus extra for dusting

1 tsp fine sea salt

FOR THE PAN SAUCE:

a knob of butter

juice of ½ lemon

freshly ground black pepper

FOR THE RICOTTA:

1 litre surplus or expired milk

80ml apple cider vinegar

juice of 1 lemon

a pinch of fine sea salt

8 fresh basil leaves, shredded, plus extra to garnish

To make the ricotta, slowly heat your milk in a saucepan until it begins to foam but not boil. Remove the pan from the heat and stir in the vinegar, lemon juice and salt. Leave it in the pan for 10 minutes, until it separates into curds.

Line a fine mesh sieve with a piece of cheesecloth or thin muslin and set the sieve over a large bowl. Pour the curdled milk into the lined sieve and leave it for 15 minutes to strain off the whey. (Don't throw away the whey! See the tip.) Transfer to a clean bowl or jar and add the fresh basil (or your favourite herbs) for extra flavour. The ricotta will keep in your fridge for up to a week.

To make the gnocchi, lightly dust a work surface with flour. Put the mashed potatoes in a large bowl and mix in the beaten egg. Stir the flour and salt together, then add to the mashed potatoes. Lightly mix with your hands until the flour and potato start to come together – the dough will still be a bit crumbly at this point. Gather it all together and press it against the bottom of the bowl until you have a smooth dough.

Tip the dough out onto the floured work surface. Using the palms of both hands, roll the dough into a rope about 2cm in diameter. With a sharp knife, cut into 2cm-thick pieces to make roughly 2cm square gnocchi. Press gently on each gnoccho with the back of a fork to form grooves on one side.

Bring a large pot of salted water to the boil. Add the gnocchi and cook for 2 minutes, just until the gnocchi float to the top. Drain.

DON'T THROW AWAY THE WHEY!

Make sure to keep the whey from making the ricotta. You can use it to make the bread on page 28 or see page 29 for other uses.

To make an easy pan sauce, melt the butter in a large frying pan over a medium heat. Add the gnocchi and fry for a few minutes, until golden on both sides. Season with salt and pepper and squeeze in the lemon juice.

To serve, divide the gnocchi between four plates. Add small spoonfuls of ricotta on top, then scatter over some shredded fresh basil.

WHEY HEY HEY BREAD

MAKES 1 LOAF

Years ago, I was at a meeting with a group of chefs in London. We were given bottles of whey vodka to try, and try we did. A certain chef who runs one of the top restaurants in London (she shall remain nameless to protect her hangover) was sitting next to me and said, 'Let's give it a go.' Each time we poured a shot, we would toast 'whey hey hey!' and then down the hatch.

When we were halfway through the bottle, I began to think about whey (don't judge me) and how it could be used in my everyday cooking. So now I use it in all sorts of ways (see the next page).

450ml whey, gently warmed

1 x 7g sachet of dried fast action yeast

1 tbsp caster sugar

625g strong white flour, plus extra for dusting

3 tbsp rapeseed oil, plus extra for greasing

2 tsp fine sea salt

Put half of the warm whey in the bowl of a stand mixer fitted with the dough hook, then add the yeast and sugar. Give it a quick stir and set aside for about 10 minutes, until the yeast starts to froth slightly.

Sift the flour into the bowl, then add the rest of the whey along with the oil and salt. Turn on the mixer to a low speed (or knead by hand) for about 3 minutes, until the dough is soft and slightly sticky. Cover the bowl with a clean cloth or tea towel and leave in a warm, draught-free place for 1–1½ hours, until the dough has doubled in size.

Grease a 900g (2lb) loaf tin with a little oil. Tip the dough out onto a lightly floured worktop and gently knead with your hands to shape it into a loaf. Put it in the tin, cover again with the cloth or tea towel and leave for another 30 minutes in a warm place, until it has risen just above the level of the tin.

Preheat the oven to 240°C (220°C fan).

Bake the loaf in the preheated oven for 10 minutes, then reduce the temperature to 220°C (200°C fan) and bake for another 20 minutes. Remove the bread from the oven and leave it in the tin for 5 minutes, then remove it from the tin and cool completely on a wire rack before cutting into slices.

WHEY

Whey is the liquid that's left over after milk has been curdled, like when you make homemade ricotta (page 26), or when yogurt has been strained to make labneh (page 6). It's an excellent source of protein and can be added to many dishes that use dairy.

1 OVERNIGHT OATS
Normally when I'm soaking oats I use apple or orange juice for flavour, but you can substitute half the amount of fruit juice for whey to pack in extra protein that will set you up for the day.

2 SMOOTHIES
Just like with the overnight oats, when making smoothies, swap out half the juice for whey for added protein.

3 PICKLES
Lactoferments and pickles help to keep your good gut bacteria happy and they also taste great. For extra goodness, you can substitute whey for one-quarter of the liquid in your pickling recipe.

4 BREAD
Using whey instead of water in a bread recipe adds depth of flavour to your loaf. I find it works really well when making a brown soda bread – it makes it richer in flavour and texture.

5 SOUPS
Replace one-quarter of the stock in a soup with whey to add extra creaminess and flavour.

REGROW FOOD

One thing I can't do is gardening. I've tried and failed on many occasions, but it's a challenge that I'm still determined to overcome in the future. However, there are simple ways to regrow food that you normally throw away, regardless of whether you have a garden or a green thumb. You can regrow food on your kitchen windowsill or an apartment balcony.

SPRING ONIONS

Spring onions can be regrown without any soil in about two weeks. When slicing your spring onions, leave about 2.5cm of the root end, then simply put it in a small jar or cup. Pour in enough water to cover the 'hairy' part of the root. If you need to stabilise it more, you can put a toothpick through the top of the spring onion and put this across the top of the jar or cup so that only the bottom part is in the water. Put in your kitchen window and watch it grow back.

LETTUCE

Regardless of the type of lettuce, if you are buying whole heads, remove all the leaves and just leave the root and about 2.5cm of the inner leaves. Regrow the lettuce the same way that you would spring onions. This will grow back into a full head of lettuce.

PAK CHOI

I don't know about you, but I find myself using pak choi more and more. Regrowing it works the same as celery (see opposite): keep the root whole and break off the outer leaves for cooking until you're left with only the small centre leaves. Put in a jar with enough water to cover the root. Leave it in your kitchen window until it starts to grow in the centre again, then transfer to a small pot with soil and look after it.

CELERY

Celery is somewhat of a Marmite vegetable – you either love it or hate it. But for those of us who like to cook with it, you can get it to regrow again and again.

When slicing your celery, leave about 5cm at the bottom that holds it all together. Turn it upside down and you'll see a small circle in the centre. Simply slice 1mm off this to expose the root.

Get a glass jar or plant pot that's big enough for the celery to fit halfway into. Pour cold water into the jar or pot until there is enough to ensure it reaches the root but does not totally immerse all the celery.

Sit the celery into the jar or pot of water and leave it in your kitchen window for about two weeks. You will start to see new celery stalks growing from the centre of the root. When this happens, transfer the root to a slightly bigger plant pot with soil. Ensure the root is deep enough in the pot and soil to cover the older part of the celery. Put it back in your window, water it once a week and watch as it grows into another full celery. Then simply reuse and repeat.

CARROT & CHILLI SCOTCH EGGS

MAKES 4

Scotch eggs were made popular by the Fortnum & Mason department store in London way back in the 1700s as food on the go for travellers. I've swapped out the sausage in the traditional recipe for surplus carrots to create a fab veggie version (or try Russell Alford and Patrick Hanlon's black pudding Scotch egg in *Blasta Books #2: Hot Fat* – definitely not vegetarian, but black pudding is in keeping with a no-waste ethos). With piccalilli on the side, it's the ultimate snack.

5 large eggs

1 tbsp rapeseed oil

½ onion, chopped

1 garlic clove, chopped

150g grated carrots (you can keep the skin on)

2 fresh red chillies, chopped

2 tbsp curry paste

100g breadcrumbs

fine sea salt and freshly ground black pepper

rapeseed or sunflower oil, for deep-frying

TO COAT:

50g plain flour

1 egg, beaten

50g breadcrumbs

a handful of fresh coriander, finely chopped

TO SERVE:

piccalilli (page 15)

Bring a pot of cold water to the boil. Working with one at a time, use a spoon to gently lower four of the eggs into the water. Boil for exactly 5 minutes, then drain and cool in a bowl of iced water or under the cold tap. When the eggs are cool enough to handle, peel off the shells and put them in your compost bin.

Heat the oil in a large frying pan over a low heat. Add the onion and garlic and cook gently for about 5 minutes, until soft, then add the grated carrots and chopped chillies and cook for 5 minutes more, until soft. Stir in the curry paste and cook for a few minutes more to release the flavours.

Transfer the onion and carrot mixture to a large bowl, stir in the breadcrumbs and season with salt and pepper. Allow to cool, then beat the remaining egg, add it to the bowl and stir everything together until it forms a paste.

Wet your hands, then divide the mixture into four equal portions. Working with one portion at a time, flatten it with your hands to form a burger shape. Put an egg in the centre and carefully wrap the mixture around it until the egg is completely covered. Put the eggs in the fridge for at least 1 hour to firm up.

Heat the oil in your deep-fryer to 180°C (or see the note).

Get three wide, shallow bowls. Put the flour in the first bowl, the beaten egg in the second bowl and the breadcrumbs mixed with the chopped fresh coriander in the third.

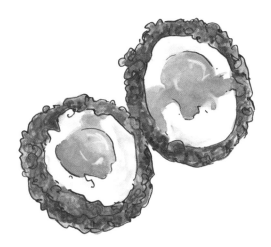

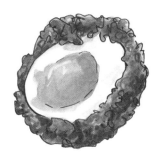

NO DEEP-FRYER? NO PROBLEM

If you don't have a deep-fryer, use a deep pot with enough oil (1–2 litres) to cover what you're frying, but make sure your pot is no more than half-full of oil.

Using your left hand, coat each Scotch egg completely in flour, then transfer it to the beaten egg. Now using your right hand, coat the Scotch egg completely in the beaten egg before transferring it to the breadcrumbs. Finally, using your left hand again, coat the egg completely in breadcrumbs. (You can leave the Scotch eggs in the fridge at this point if you're making them in advance.)

Gently lower the Scotch eggs into the deep-fryer and cook for 7 minutes, turning occasionally, until golden. Use a large slotted spoon to transfer to a plate lined with kitchen paper to drain off any excess oil.

To serve, cut each Scotch egg in half lengthways. Put on a plate and add a few spoonfuls of piccalilli on the side.

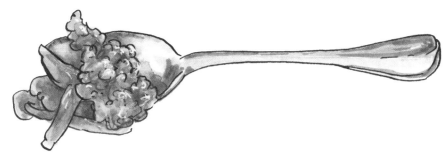

VEGETABLE RAMEN

SERVES 2

One of my absolute favourite dishes is ramen. This version is a brilliant way to use up all types of veg in your fridge – spinach, red onions, carrots, spring onions, mushrooms – so don't feel limited by what I've used here.

The most important part of any ramen is the stock or base. After you get that right, then it's just a matter of adding what you like. Served with noodles, a soft-boiled egg and your favourite vegetables, this recipe is a must-have in your no-waste repertoire.

2 eggs

300g dried noodles (or leftover cooked noodles – see the tip on page 25)

rapeseed oil, for cooking

2 garlic cloves, crushed

a thumb-sized piece of fresh ginger, finely grated

5g dried mushrooms

2 sheets of nori seaweed, cut into small strips

1 litre homemade vegetable stock (page 23)

1 tbsp soy sauce

2 tbsp miso paste

1 head of pak choi, quartered lengthways

100g mangetout

2 carrots, peeled into ribbons

2 spring onions, thinly sliced at an angle

1 small bunch of fresh coriander, chopped

chilli oil (page 44 or shop-bought)

Bring a small pot of cold water to the boil. Put each egg on a spoon and gently lower it into the pot. Boil for exactly 6 minutes, then drain and cool in a bowl of iced water or under the cold tap. When the eggs are cool enough to handle, peel off the shells and put them in your compost bin.

Meanwhile, bring a separate pot of water to the boil. Add the noodles and cook according to the packet instructions, then drain and set aside.

Heat some rapeseed oil in a large pot set on a low heat. Add the garlic and ginger and cook, stirring, for 2 minutes. Add the dried mushrooms and cook for another minute before adding the nori, vegetable stock and soy sauce. Bring to a simmer and gently cook for 10 minutes to infuse the flavours. Stir in the miso paste, then add the pak choi, mangetout and cooked noodles. Simmer for 2 minutes, until the vegetables are cooked through.

Divide the noodles, vegetables and broth between two deep bowls. Gently put the halved soft-boiled eggs on top, then finish with the carrot ribbons, spring onions and chopped fresh coriander. Drizzle with some chilli oil for an extra kick.

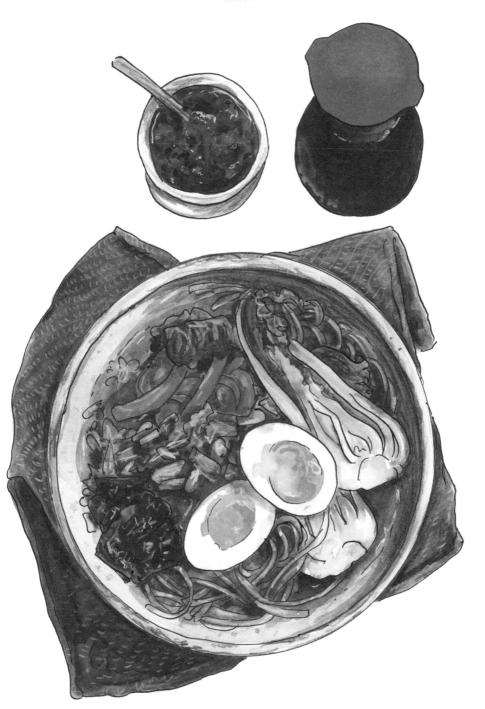

BROCCOLI STALKS

1 PESTO

The word 'pesto' comes from the Italian verb 'pestare', which means 'to pound' or 'to crush', so you don't have to stick to the usual basil, Parmesan and pine nuts. Chop your broccoli, including the stalks and leaves, into very small pieces, then substitute half the amount of basil for broccoli. It adds depth of flavour and is great poured over pasta or salads.

2 BROCCOLI STALK SLAW

Replace the cabbage in a traditional coleslaw with broccoli stalks – it tastes even better than the original. Grate your stalks into a bowl, then add grated carrots and season with sea salt and coarsely ground black pepper. I love to use half mayonnaise and half natural yogurt in the dressing for a better texture and background flavour.

3 STIR-FRY

Broccoli stalks and leaves are a great addition to a stir-fry. Slice the stalks thinly (no need to peel them) and add to your wok or pan towards the end of the cooking so that they still have a bit of a bite to them. They pair really well with soy sauce and chilli.

4 ROAST STALKS & DUKKAH

Broccoli stalks make a fantastic roast veg to accompany any meal – trust me on this. Preheat your oven to 210°C (190°C fan). Slice the stalks in half lengthways and put them in a bowl. Drizzle with rapeseed oil and season with coarse sea salt, then use your hands to toss and coat them all over. Put on a baking tray and into the preheated oven for 10–15 minutes, until tender. I top them with dukkah (page 6) or chopped roasted nuts. A drizzle of natural yogurt is great too.

5 SOUP

A bit more of a traditional way to use broccoli in its entirety, but definitely a tasty one. Slice the stalks separately to the head. Cook them at the beginning with onions and garlic to really release the flavour, then add the florets before pouring in vegetable stock and blending when cooked. This is great served with a spoonful of the broccoli pesto on top.

POTATO HASH WITH BROCCOMOLI

SERVES 4

Now that everyone wants avocados smashed on everything, it's had a big environmental impact. The increased demand for avocados has led to increased deforestation, which in turn leads to increased global warming and climate change. The good news is that you don't need to use avocados to create a delicious (and climate-friendly!) dip – broccoli will do the job.

Looking into my cupboards and fridge and seeing a few potatoes, an onion, a couple sad cloves of garlic and some unloved bits of veg, this is my go-to lunch. This hash always changes depending on what I need to use up, but potatoes are always used as the base.

700g potatoes, unpeeled and cut into wedges

2 tbsp paprika

rapeseed oil

fine sea salt and freshly ground black pepper

1 white or red onion, halved and sliced

1 pepper (any colour), sliced

2 garlic cloves, crushed

½ bag of leaves (spinach, rocket, etc.)

2 spring onions, thinly sliced at an angle

FOR THE BROCCOMOLI:

200g broccoli florets and stalks, finely chopped

½ onion, finely chopped

1 fresh red chilli, chopped

½ bunch of fresh coriander, chopped

juice of 2 lemons

fine sea salt and freshly ground black pepper

Preheat the oven to 210°C (190°C fan).

To make the broccomoli, bring a pot of water to the boil. Add the broccoli florets and stalks and blanch for 2 minutes, then drain and refresh under cold running water to stop them cooking. Drain again, put in a blender or food processor and pulse into a paste. Add the onion, chilli, coriander and lemon juice and blend into your desired consistency (I like mine chunky). Season with salt and pepper and that's it. Set aside.

To make the hash, put the potato wedges in a bowl with the paprika, a drizzle of rapeseed oil and a pinch of salt and pepper. Toss with your hands to ensure all the wedges are coated, then spread them out on a baking tray and roast in the preheated oven for 10 minutes.

Remove the tray from the oven and add the onion, pepper and garlic. Mix them through the wedges with a spoon, then put the tray back in the oven and roast for another 10 minutes, until the wedges and veg are cooked and slightly charred. Remove the tray from the oven again, add the leaves and spring onions and fold them through.

To serve, divide everything between four plates and add a spoonful of broccomoli on top of each portion. This is also great with a crispy fried egg (see page 20).

MAKE YOUR OWN YOGURT

It's so easy to make yogurt at home using shop-bought yogurt. This way, you only ever have to buy it once and after that you can make your own. It's like the yogurt equivalent of regrowing veg (see pages 30–31).

1 To begin with, buy a natural yogurt that says 'live' or 'cultured' on the label to ensure it contains living cultures.

4 Eat and repeat!

2 When you get down to the last few spoonfuls in the tub, slowly heat 1 litre of full-fat milk in a saucepan over a medium heat until it starts to foam slightly, but do not let it boil. Take the pan off the heat and allow it to cool to room temperature.

3 Once cooled, stir in 120ml of your live or cultured yogurt. Cover the pan with a lid and leave it in a warm place overnight – a hot press would be perfect. The next day you'll have delicious thick yogurt all over again.

CAULIFLOWER BHAJIS WITH CORIANDER YOGURT & FLATBREADS

SERVES 2 AS A MAIN OR 4 AS A STARTER

My no-waste take on a classic Indian onion bhaji uses the leaves and stalks from a head of cauliflower, combined with a coriander yogurt as a dipping sauce and flatbreads to mop up all the flavours on the plate.

FOR THE BHAJIS:

100g cauliflower leaves and stalks

100g sliced red onion

100g self-raising flour

½ tsp baking powder

½ tsp chilli powder

½ tsp ground coriander

½ tsp ground turmeric

150ml cold water

fine sea salt and freshly ground black pepper

rapeseed or sunflower oil, for frying

FOR THE CORIANDER YOGURT:

a handful of fresh coriander, finely chopped, plus extra to garnish

150g homemade (page 39) or natural yogurt

FOR THE FLATBREADS:

200g plain flour, plus extra for dusting

100ml warm water

1 tbsp rapeseed oil

To make the coriander yogurt, simply mix the chopped coriander into the yogurt and season it with some cracked black pepper. Set aside to let the flavours marry together.

To make the bhajis, keep the top of the cauliflower leaves and the smaller leaves whole and add them to a bowl with the thinly sliced red onion. Thinly slice the thicker stalks and bigger leaves, then add them to the bowl too.

Put the flour, baking powder and spices in a separate bowl and whisk to combine. Slowly add the water with one hand while whisking at the same time with your other hand. Once all the water has been added, whisk into a smooth batter and season with salt and pepper. Pour the batter over the cauliflower and onion and mix until evenly combined.

Heat 2.5cm worth of oil in a large non-stick frying pan. If you have a thermometer, it should be 180°C. If you don't have one, you can test the temperature by dropping a cube of bread into the hot oil – if it turns golden brown in 1 minute, it's just right.

Using a dessertspoon, carefully and gently drop spoonfuls of the bhaji mixture into the hot oil. Make sure to do this in batches so that you don't cook too many at once, otherwise they'll stick together. You should get around 10 bhajis in total.

Shallow-fry for 2 minutes, then turn them over and fry for a further 2 minutes. Remove with a slotted spoon onto a plate lined with kitchen paper to absorb any excess oil. Keep warm in a low oven while you make the flatbreads.

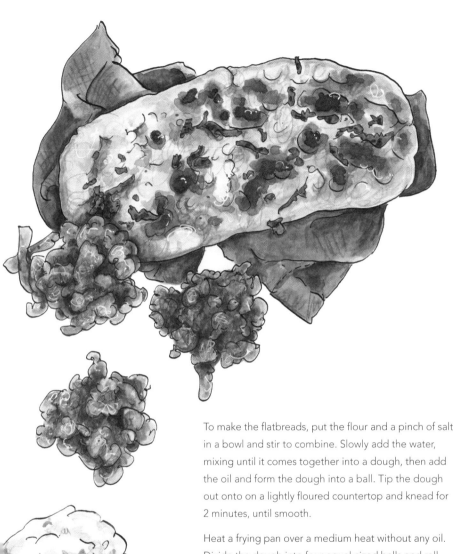

To make the flatbreads, put the flour and a pinch of salt in a bowl and stir to combine. Slowly add the water, mixing until it comes together into a dough, then add the oil and form the dough into a ball. Tip the dough out onto on a lightly floured countertop and knead for 2 minutes, until smooth.

Heat a frying pan over a medium heat without any oil. Divide the dough into four equal-sized balls and roll each one out into a 1cm-thick oval. Add one or two flatbreads to the hot pan and cook for 2 minutes on each side.

To serve, divide the flatbreads between your plates and put the bhajis on top. Scatter over a little finely chopped fresh coriander to garnish, then add the coriander yogurt on the side as a dipping sauce.

ALL ABOUT
AQUAFABA

Don't throw away the water from a tin or jar of chickpeas! It's called aquafaba (aqua = water, faba = bean) and you can use it as a substitute for egg whites in vegan dishes. The aquafaba won't replace the proteins from eggs, but it will add vitamin B, iron and healthy fatty acids.

It's important to note, though, that when you see recipes referring to aquafaba, it's from chickpeas only. Water from other tins of beans doesn't work the same way.

You can freeze aquafaba. Just spoon it into an ice cube tray, then pop out the cubes once they're frozen solid and store them in a freezerproof bag for up to four months.

1 MERINGUES OR PAVLOVA

Believe it or not, aquafaba makes fantastic vegan meringues. Using the same recipe and method as for regular meringues, you can swap out each egg white for 2 tablespoons of aquafaba and get a delicious dessert.

2 WHIPPED CREAM

If you're vegan and missing the flavour and texture of whipped cream with desserts, then aquafaba works wonders here too. Whip the aquafaba to form stiff peaks, then add icing sugar to sweeten and a squeeze of lemon juice to stabilise it.

3 MAYONNAISE

I find that a vegan mayonnaise is actually much creamier and lighter than a traditional mayo made using egg yolks. Just use 1 tablespoon of aquafaba in place of one egg yolk in your usual recipe.

1 tablespoon aquafaba = 1 egg yolk
2 tablespoons aquafaba = 1 egg white
3 tablespoons aquafaba = 1 whole egg

ROAST CABBAGE WEDGES WITH HUMMUS, PEANUTS & CHILLI OIL

SERVES 2

Is it just me or do you also have childhood memories of cabbage being boiled for hours, until it got to the stage where it dissolved on your tongue? And because it was always cooked in ham or bacon water, that was pretty much all it tasted of. It wasn't the cabbage's fault. This recipe makes cabbage cool again.

When buying a head of cabbage I never use it all in one dish, so this recipe uses that half a head that's lying in the back of the fridge. You can buy hummus in most shops these days, but it's so quick and easy to make it yourself. As for the chilli oil, I always look for oils that are grown and produced here in Ireland, so that means rapeseed oils will always win over imported oils. There are some excellent flavoured oils available now, so you could simply buy a good chilli rapeseed oil. But if you have some chillies left over, you can make your own to add to your zero-waste larder.

½ head of cabbage, cut into 4 x 90g wedges

fine sea salt and freshly ground black pepper

2 tsp chilli powder

2 tsp paprika

50g peanuts, roughly chopped

FOR THE HUMMUS:

1 x 400g tin of chickpeas

1 garlic clove, crushed

juice of 1 lemon

3 tbsp tahini

FOR THE CHILLI OIL:

450ml rapeseed oil

3 fresh red or green chillies

15g chilli flakes

First, make the chilli oil. Gently warm the rapeseed oil in a pot over a low heat. Add the whole chillies and the chilli flakes and heat for 3–4 minutes. Remove the pot from the heat and let the oil cool overnight to infuse. The next day, strain it into a sterilised glass bottle (see page 51) through a fine mesh sieve and discard the chilli flakes, then add the whole chillies to the bottle and seal it. Store the bottle in the refrigerator and use the oil within two weeks.

To make your own hummus, set a colander over a bowl. Drain the chickpeas but keep the water from the tin (this is called aquafaba – see pages 42–43). Put the chickpeas in a food processor with half of the aquafaba and blend to combine. Add the garlic, lemon juice and tahini and blend again. If the consistency is too thick, gradually add some water until it becomes smooth. Season with salt and pepper and you're good to go.

Preheat the oven to 210°C (190°C fan).

Put the cabbage wedges on a baking tray, drizzle with the chilli oil and season with salt and pepper. Roast on the middle shelf of the preheated oven for 10 minutes.

Remove the tray from the oven and spread some hummus onto one side of each cabbage wedge. Mix the chilli powder and paprika together, then sprinkle it over the hummus-coated side. Scatter the peanuts around the base of the cabbage, then put the tray back in the oven to roast for another 10 minutes, until the cabbage is just tender.

To serve, put two wedges on each plate, hummus side facing up, then spoon over the roasted peanuts from the baking tray and drizzle some chilli oil over everything. I love this as a lunch dish served with salad and feta cheese.

FIVE WAYS WITH

FIVE WAYS WITH
FERMENTATION

Fermentation can seem a bit daunting, but a few basic recipes can be easily made at home. Not only does fermented food feed your good gut bacteria, but it also adds fantastic flavours to dishes and uses fruit and vegetables that normally get thrown away.

1 CULTURED VINEGAR

This is a real vinegar made from fruit skins – not the type for your chips! – and gives you another fantastic condiment to add to your waste-free larder rather than sending your fruit skins straight to the compost heap.

Get a large Kilner jar, one big enough to hold all your fruit skins (my favourites are apple and melon – if you're using apples, add the cores too). Put all the fruit skins in the jar – the jar should be at least half full. Add 2 dessertspoons of sugar and pour in enough cold water to completely cover everything. Put a weight on top – a small saucer will do the job – so that everything is kept submerged. Cover the jar with a clean cloth or tea towel, secure it with a rubber band and leave the jar in a cool, dark cupboard for up to four weeks. Each week, you need to clean the top of the jar and remove any foam, etc. that may have appeared. After the four weeks, strain the vinegar through a fine mesh sieve to remove all the skins for compost, then pour into a clean bottle and seal. This will keep for over a year and is great in dressings. You can also add a dash to sauces for extra flavour and acidity.

2 KIMCHI

Kimchi is a great way to start fermenting at home. It's my favourite, so I always have some on hand to add a kick to any dish. The traditional Korean kimchi dates back thousands of years and many families have passed their recipes down through the generations. I've adapted the traditional recipe to incorporate lots of fruit and vegetables that are often left languishing in the fridge and cupboards, and I've also removed the fermented fish sauce to keep it vegetarian. The recipe for my empty-the-fridge kimchi is on page 52 and I also love to add it to a cheese toastie (page 56).

3 KOSHO

Kosho is a Japanese seasoning with a umami explosion. The word 'kosho' means 'pepper' in Japanese, referring to the chilli pepper it's made with. Traditionally it's made using yuzu, a citrus fruit found in East Asia that's hard to get here, so I swap it out for lemons, limes or grapefruits. Once you make this and have it in your fridge, you'll become addicted to it. Kosho is a great way to cut through the richness of many dishes, from meat to noodles and everything in between – I use it to add a kick to pasta with wild mushrooms (page 60).

To make kosho, halve 6 red chillies lengthways and remove the seeds. Cut them into chunks, put them in a blender or food processer and pulse until they are finely chopped. Zest the citrus fruit you need to use up (either 4 lemons, 3 oranges or 1 grapefruit) and add it to the blender or food processor. Pulse until it's well mixed with the chillies, then add 16g flaky sea salt and pulse again until it forms a paste. This is ready to use straightaway, but I like to put it into an airtight jar and leave it at room temperature for one week to slightly ferment and take on more flavour. Store the kosho in a sealed jar in your fridge, where it will keep for up to three months.

4 KOMBUCHA & KEFIR

For me, this ancient drink of fermented tea is the king of culture. But to make it, you need a scoby (symbiotic culture of bacteria and yeast). You can spend months growing one from scratch or you can take the easier route and either hit up a friend who makes kombucha or buy one online.

Purists insist on kombucha being made with the best organic teas and some insist on leaf tea only, but I've always used regular tea bags and sugar. Basically, what you are doing here is making/brewing a sweet tea. My basic recipe ratio is 1 litre water, 100g sugar and 4 tea bags (you can scale this up according to the size of your jar). It's as easy as boiling the kettle, putting the sugar and tea bags in a large heatproof bowl, pouring over the litre of boiling water and stirring until the sugar has dissolved. Once it's cooled to room temperature, remove the tea bags and pour into a large, clean Kilner jar. Add your scoby and a cup of kombucha (either from a previous homemade batch or shop-bought) and cover the top of the jar with a clean cloth secured with a rubber band. Leave the jar in a warm area but kept out of sunlight for seven days. Remove the scoby and put it into another jar with a cup of this newly brewed kombucha. Seal the jar and leave it in a dark cupboard until you are ready to make another batch.

This is the stage where surplus ingredients come in. In the summertime I add over-ripe berries to the kombucha (about ½ cup per litre), but you can use any kind of fruit. This time, seal the jar with a lid after you add the berries and leave it for another seven days. Now it will take on the flavour of the berries and self-carbonate into a wonderfully fizzy, refreshing drink. Remove the berries, then bottle up the booch and enjoy. But we are not finished with the berries yet!

Milk kefir is the end-of-the-line recipe that I always turn to for the berries or fruits I've used in my kombucha to ensure there is absolutely no waste. I use the kefir like yogurt, blending it with the kombucha fruit to create smoothies and great drinks. A bit more tender loving care is involved in making a kefir with kefir grains compared to a kombucha scoby, but your kefir will be ready within 48 hours. Similar to a scoby, it's always good to hit up a friend who is making kefir for their grains or you can buy the grains in health food shops. Shop-bought grains come in a small sachet and will need to be brought back to life to get going. It's definitely worth giving it a go.

Put ½ teaspoon kefir grains in a 1-litre sterilised Kilner jar (see page 51). Pour in 600ml milk, cover the top of the jar with a clean cloth and secure with a rubber band. Leave the jar on your kitchen counter for 24 hours to ferment. It will thicken into a yogurt consistency. Strain the kefir through a sieve, pour into a bottle and store in your fridge. It will keep for two weeks. Put the grains back into a clean jar and start again. If you want to take a break from making kefir, you can store the grains in your fridge for three weeks and then start the process again.

5 SAUERKRAUT

Sauerkraut is fermented cabbage and I always have a jar of it in the fridge. I use it in everything from toasties and fritters to condiments for serving with cheese.

To make one large jar (850ml), you need 1kg white cabbage, 3 tablespoons flaky sea salt, ½ teaspoon caraway seeds and ½ teaspoon peppercorns. Finely shred the cabbage and put it in a large bowl. Sprinkle over the salt, then massage it into the cabbage for a few minutes. Leave it for 10 minutes, then massage it again and leave it for another 10 minutes. By now, the salt should have drawn the water out of the cabbage to create a brine. Mix in the caraway seeds and peppercorns, then transfer the cabbage to a 1-litre Kilner jar. As you are putting the cabbage into the jar, make sure you press it down firmly so that the brine completely covers the cabbage. When you've filled the jar, put a weight on top or use some whole cabbage leaves so that the cabbage stays completely submerged. Seal the jar and leave it at room temperature for a week, by which time you should start to see bubbles on the side of the jar. Put the jar in your fridge and you're ready to go. The sauerkraut will keep for up to four weeks in the fridge.

FERMENTATION
TOP TIPS

----

1 STERILISE

It's important to sterilise your jars and cooking equipment before use to reduce the risk of bad bacteria contaminating your ferment. The easiest way to do this is to wash your jars, lids and utensils in a dishwasher. Alternatively, wash everything in hot soapy water, rinse well, then put the jars on a baking tray and pop them into the oven at 140°C (120°C fan) to dry out completely. If you're using jars with a rubber ring seal, boil the seals in a small saucepan for 2–3 minutes – do not put them in the oven, as the heat will damage them.

2 SUBMERGE

When we talk about fermentation, the majority is what's known as lactofermentation. Basically, the food must be kept submerged in liquid. This prevents the growth of bad bacteria (as they cannot survive without oxygen), which in turn prevents the food from spoiling. You can simply weigh down the ingredients using a saucer, a small plate or a weight that fits inside your jar. For serial fermenters, you can buy glass weights online especially for this purpose.

3 LEAVE ROOM

When filling your jars with ferments, always leave about 2.5cm clear at the top of the jar. During the fermentation process the food can expand and needs some room, but as mentioned above, ensure that the ferment is totally submerged at all times.

4 AVOID A MESS

When making ferments, I always put the jars on a plate. As the gas builds up in the jar, the liquid can sometimes spill out over the lid and onto your counter. It's also important to 'burp' some ferments, such as kimchi, sauerkraut and kombucha, to release the build-up of gases in the jar. I slowly open each jar once a week to release the gas, then seal it again.

5 STORE

When you've tasted your ferment and are happy with the flavours, you need to transfer it to your fridge. This will slow down the fermentation process and keep it at the flavour you like, but it won't stop the process entirely.

EMPTY-THE-FRIDGE KIMCHI

MAKES 1 MEDIUM JAR

This is not an authentic kimchi, but hear me out. The traditional Korean recipe goes back centuries, but I've taken the idea and used a similar process, omitting the fermented fish sauce but keeping the fantastic spicy kick.

Kimchi is a great way to use bits and ends of vegetables and fruits before getting your next shop in. It's packed with flavour and is great in stir-frys, salads, omelettes, pastas, fried rice … pretty much anything you can think of (try it in the kimchi toastie on page 56). I find that once you introduce kimchi to your diet, you wonder how you're only just discovering it now.

1 Chinese cabbage or any soft green cabbage

approx. 20g fine sea salt

1 carrot

leftover pieces of onion, diced into small pieces

leftover trimmings from celery or any raw vegetables, diced into small pieces

roots and leaves from cauliflower and/or broccoli, diced into small pieces

leftover green beans or mangetout, diced into small pieces

1 apple (it's okay if it's bruised)

2 garlic cloves, peeled and left whole

a thumb-sized piece of fresh ginger (no need to peel)

2 dessertspoons chilli powder

Weigh your cabbage and work out a 2% salt-to-cabbage ratio. For example, a typical head of cabbage weighs around 1kg, so you would need 20g salt.

Slice the cabbage and put it in a large bowl. Gently massage the salt into the cabbage, then set it aside for about 30 minutes to let the salt draw out the water in the cabbage and begin the brine.

Give your carrot a good scrub (I leave the skin on for this), then grate it into a large bowl. Add the other leftover raw vegetables that you're using.

Put the apple, garlic, ginger and chilli powder in a blender. Add a splash of water and blitz into a paste, then gradually add a little more water and blend again until you get a thin soup-like consistency.

At this stage the liquid should have been drawn out of the cabbage, so add all the raw vegetables and toss to combine, then add the chilli paste. Massage everything together and transfer to a large sterilised jar (see page 51). As you are putting the kimchi into the jar, keep pushing down on it until it's submerged in liquid – this is an important part of the lactofermentation process, as it ensures mould and bad bacteria can't grow here. If needed, you can top up the jar with water to make sure everything is completely submerged (see page 51).

FUNKYTOWN

Taste the kimchi after six days to see if you like the flavour, but you can absolutely leave it out on the counter to ferment for longer for a funkier, stronger flavour.

Cover the jar with a lid and leave it on your kitchen counter for at least six days. After a couple of days, you should start to see bubbles on the side of the jar – this is good! It means that fermentation is happening. If you're happy with the flavour after six days (or see the tip), put it in the fridge, where it will keep for a month – but I'm sure you'll have eaten it all well before then.

FIVE WAYS WITH
CHEESE

My guilty pleasure is cheese. I love it and always have a few different types in my fridge, but this means that I often end up with the ends of various cheeses that have gone hard. In this book, I've put those odds and ends to good use in the kimchi toastie (page 56) and cheese fritters (page 24), but here are some other ideas for how to use them up.

1 PARMESAN RINDS

Toasted Parmesan rinds are like a bacon substitute that you can use in all sorts of ways – I add them to pasta with mushrooms and kosho (page 60). Or add them just as they are, untoasted, to soups while they simmer for extra flavour. Store them in an airtight container in the fridge or in a freezerproof bag in the freezer.

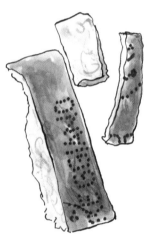

2 MAC 'N' CHEESE

I know it's mac 'n' cheese time when I have a collection of cheeses in my fridge. As a rule, I use softer cheeses (Brie, goat cheese, cream cheese, etc.) in the sauce and keep the harder cheeses such as Parmesan for the top to create a delicious crust with breadcrumbs.

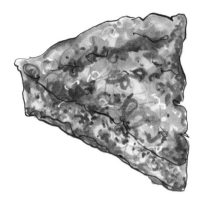

3 QUICHE OR TARTS

Spread some chutney on a shortcrust pastry base, then onion jam, then crumbled or grated cheeses. Add beaten eggs and slowly bake into deliciousness for a great summertime lunch.

4 FLATBREADS

The recipe on page 40 for homemade flatbreads can also be used to make a cheesy snack. Put the cooked flatbreads on a baking tray, top with pieces of surplus cheese and pop under a hot grill for 2–3 minutes to melt, then drizzle over some carrot top pesto (page 6).

5 CAULIFLOWER CHEESE

The strong flavour of cauliflower allows you to pair it with different types of cheese. My favourite version is to use the recipe from page 56 for the cheesy rarebit sauce. Add blanched cauliflower to a baking dish, cover in the sauce and top with even more cheese bits. Bake in the oven at 200°C (180°C fan) for 20 minutes, until golden, melted and gooey.

CHEESY KIMCHI TOASTIE WITH BLOODY MARY MAYO
(THE MORNING AFTER THE NIGHT BEFORE)

MAKES 1

This is my ultimate quick and easy brunch, lunch (I'm never sure what the difference is) or hangover cure. Of course, that's assuming that you're organised and have the components already made and ready to go as part of your no-waste kitchen.

I haven't reinvented the wheel here – this recipe is based on the classic Welsh rarebit. It was one of the first dishes I learned as a commis chef many moons ago in London. As for the mayo, there is no vodka in it, but it does have the same spicy kick as a great Bloody Mary. Depending on your mood or how bad your hangover is, you can use your favourite shop-bought mayo or you can make it from scratch in minutes.

With your jar of kimchi and your cheesy bits already at hand, you just need to head out to your local bakery for a fresh loaf of sourdough – and a strong coffee for the trip back. The rest is simple.

120ml Guinness or milk

25g butter, plus extra softened butter for spreading

25g plain flour

140g cheese ends (you can use any odds and ends here – I normally have a mix of soft and hard cheeses), roughly chopped or grated

1 tbsp Worcestershire sauce

1 tsp prepared English mustard

1 egg yolk

2 thick slices of sourdough bread

a little kimchi (page 52), chopped so it's not too chunky

First, make the mayo. If you're making it from scratch (or see the intro), using a stand mixer, blender or hand blender, whisk the egg yolks until creamy, then whisk in the mustard and salt. Very slowly – literally drop by drop – add half of the oil while continuously whisking or blending until thickened. Whisk in 1 tablespoon of vinegar to loosen the mixture slightly and give it a paler colour. Continue to add the remaining oil in a slow, steady stream, still whisking continuously. Season with another pinch of salt, a squeeze of lemon juice and another tablespoon of vinegar if needed. You now have a basic plain mayo that you can store in a sterilised jar (see page 51) in the fridge for up to one week. To make it into a Bloody Mary mayo, simply stir in some of the fantastic brine from the jar of kimchi. My ratio is two spoons of mayo to one spoon of kimchi brine.

To make the toasties, get two small saucepans. Put the Guinness or milk in one pan and slowly warm it over a medium heat.

FOR THE BLOODY MARY MAYO:

2 egg yolks (see the tip)

1 tsp English mustard

a pinch of fine sea salt

500ml rapeseed oil (or any neutral oil)

1–2 tbsp white wine vinegar

juice of ½ lemon

brine from your jar of kimchi

Melt the butter in the second saucepan, then add the flour, stir to combine and cook for about 1 minute. Gradually whisk in the warm Guinness or milk to create a smooth sauce, then add your cheese mixture. Stir with a wooden spoon until all the cheese has completely melted and you have a thick paste, then stir in the Worcestershire sauce and mustard until evenly combined. Take the pan off the heat and allow to cool slightly, then stir in the egg yolk. (You can keep this in a covered tub in your fridge at this point, ready to go for a snack of cheese on toast.)

Now it's time to bring it all together. I love copious amounts of mayo spread evenly over one side of each slice of bread, then the cheesy spread, then the kimchi. Sandwich it together, then spread some softened butter on the outside of both pieces of bread.

Put the sandwich in a warm frying pan over a medium heat (or you can use a sandwich toaster) and gently toast until the bread is golden, then carefully turn it over and toast the other side. Reduce the heat and cook each side for 1–2 minutes longer, until the centre is warm.

Dig in with a strong coffee, a lunch cocktail or a good beer to set yourself up for the rest of the day.

SAUERKRAUT FRITTERS WITH POACHED EGGS & HOMEMADE YOGURT

SERVES 2

As a young chef, I remember opening tins of sauerkraut at the back of the kitchen and loving the flavours, but I was never sure how it was made. Google didn't exist back then, so I couldn't just whip my phone out of my pocket to look it up. To learn as a chef, you had to dismantle a dish and try to recreate it using different methods and ingredients until you were happy with it.

200g sauerkraut (page 50 or shop-bought), roughly chopped

60g plain flour

1 tsp baking powder

fine sea salt and freshly ground black pepper

2 tbsp sauerkraut brine

1 tbsp rapeseed oil

2 very fresh eggs

a splash of white wine vinegar

homemade yogurt (page 39), to serve

Mix the sauerkraut, flour and baking powder together in a bowl and season with salt and pepper. Add the sauerkraut brine and mix into a thick batter.

Heat the oil in a large non-stick frying pan over a medium heat. Add spoonfuls of the mix to the pan (like potato rösti) and fry for 4–5 minutes on each side, until lightly browned. You should aim to get six fritters. Set aside and keep warm.

Meanwhile, poach your eggs. The No. 1 rule to poaching an egg is to make it's very fresh. Crack your egg into a bowl or cup to make it easier to slide into the pan. Bring a small saucepan of water to a simmer and add a splash of vinegar. Stir the water to create a gentle whirlpool in the centre, then slowly add the egg. Keep it on a low heat and cook for 3–4 minutes, then remove with a slotted spoon to a plate lined with kitchen paper. Repeat with the second egg.

To serve, put a stack of three fritters on each plate. Add a big spoonful of your homemade yogurt and put a poached egg on top.

PASTA WITH MUSHROOMS, KOSHO & TOASTED PARMESAN RIND

SERVES 2

It's definitely not traditional, but I love to use kosho, a Japanese condiment, with pasta (see page 47 for more on kosho). Mushrooms and the crispy Parmesan rind give it an extra umami boost.

20g Parmesan rind

240g shop-bought fresh pasta (spaghetti is perfect for this)

40g butter

rapeseed oil, for cooking

160g mixed fresh mushrooms, thickly sliced

3 tsp kosho (page 47)

fine sea salt and freshly ground black pepper

½ handful of fresh coriander, chopped

Preheat your grill. Put the Parmesan rinds on a baking tray, skin side up, and put the tray under your grill. Keep a close eye on them and wait until they start to bubble and colour, then remove them straightaway. Put them on a chopping board. Using a sharp knife, chop the rinds into small cubes.

Cook the pasta according to the packet instructions but reduce the cooking time by 2 minutes to keep it al dente. When the pasta is cooked, keep a mugful of the cooking water from the pot before straining the pasta.

Put the pot that you used to cook the pasta back on the hob on a medium heat. Add the butter and a splash of rapeseed oil. When the butter has melted, add the mushrooms and cook for 2 minutes, until they begin to soften. Stir in the kosho and the mugful of pasta water, then add the drained pasta, stirring to make sure the pasta is all coated in the sauce.

Check the seasoning – the kosho is quite salty and spicy so I don't add any salt throughout the cooking process, but you may like to season it to taste with salt and pepper.

To serve, divide the pasta between two wide, shallow bowls. Top with the toasted Parmesan rinds and chopped fresh coriander.

PINEAPPLE TEPACHE MARGARITA

Tepache is a classic Mexican drink made using pineapple skins. Through the natural fermentation, this will self-carbonate into a deliciously fizzy, refreshing drink that you can have on its own or as a cocktail mixer, like in this margarita. The amounts given here make 1 litre of tepache and one margarita, but just scale up the margarita quantities if you want to make a large pitcher for a party.

FOR THE TEPACHE:

1 litre water

150g light brown sugar

skin and core of 1 pineapple

1 cinnamon stick

1 chilli pepper, chopped (optional)

FOR THE MARGARITA:

ground rock salt or Tajín seasoning

1 lime wedge

ice cubes

50ml tequila

25ml tepache

20ml Triple Sec

1 fresh pineapple wedge

To make the tepache, pour the water into a pot and bring it to the boil, then add the sugar. Remove the pot from the heat and stir occasionally until the sugar has dissolved. You can either pour this into a sterilised 1-litre Kilner jar (see page 51) or leave it in the pot. Either way, add the pineapple skin and core, cinnamon stick and chopped chilli (if using). Cover the jar with a paper napkin or a thin, clean cloth secured with a rubber band. Leave the jar out at room temperature, out of direct sunlight, for 48 hours (or you can put the jar in a dark cupboard).

After 48 hours, pass through a fine mesh sieve to remove the skin and core (you can compost these now), cinnamon stick and chilli, then decant into sterilised bottles. Seal the bottles and leave for another 48 hours at room temperature to carbonate. If you won't be using the tepache straightaway, then burp the jar (see page 51) and store it in the fridge.

To make the margarita, put a few teaspoons of salt or Tajín on a small plate or saucer. Rub the lime wedge around the rim of a glass, then dip the glass into the salt or Tajín so that the entire rim is covered.

Fill a cocktail shaker with ice (or use a jug and half fill it with ice), then add the tequila, tepache and Triple Sec. Shake until the outside of the shaker feels cold (or stir well with a wooden spoon if using a pitcher). Strain into the prepared glass over fresh ice and garnish with a wedge of fresh pineapple.

CHOCOLATE CHIP & COFFEE GROUNDS COOKIES

MAKES 12

We've become a nation of coffee drinkers, and while we love our local coffee shops and baristas, many of us have brought good coffee into our homes too. This has seen us invest in coffee machines that produce fresh bean-to-cup coffee at the touch of a button. Over the years I've worked on many recipes and ideas using leftover coffee grounds – not all of them successful. The best results have been using them in soil to help grow herbs, lettuces and light salads; rebrewing them to make coffee kombucha; and a firm favourite was a coffee-flavoured pastrami. This recipe is a great way to make a delicious cookie that's good on its own or used with your favourite ice cream to make an ice cream sandwich.

75g salted butter, softened, plus extra for greasing

40g light brown muscovado sugar

1 large egg

2 tsp vanilla extract

100g plain flour

20g used coffee grounds

½ tsp baking powder

100g plain chocolate chips or chunks

flaky sea salt

Put the softened butter and brown sugar in a bowl and beat until creamy, then add the egg and vanilla extract and beat again.

Sift the flour, coffee grounds and baking powder into the bowl and mix with a wooden spoon until well combined, then add your chocolate chips or chunks and stir well. Refrigerate the dough for at least 20 minutes or overnight.

Preheat the oven to 200°C (180°C fan). Line two baking trays with non-stick baking paper. Make sure to rub some butter on the paper too.

Divide the dough into 12 even portions and roll into balls between the palms of your hands. Space the balls well apart on the baking trays, then sprinkle some flaky sea salt on top of each one.

Bake in the preheated oven for 12–15 minutes, until the cookies are baked on the edges but still slightly soft in the centres if you press them.

Leave on the tray for a couple of minutes to set, then transfer to a wire cooling rack.

BREAD & JAM PUDDING

SERVES 6

We all love a good bread and butter pudding, but this is an even older recipe that uses the jam you may have sitting in the back of your cupboard instead of butter and stale bread to create a warming, tasty dessert. What I love most about this is just how easy and rustic it is.

1 loaf of bread, whole or sliced (500g)

200g jam (any flavour)

4 large eggs

100g caster sugar

1 tsp vanilla extract

600ml milk

40g butter, plus extra for greasing

50g icing sugar

TO SERVE:

custard, ice cream or cream

Preheat the oven to 210°C (190°C fan). Grease a 23cm x 33cm baking dish with butter.

Cut or tear your bread in half. Put one half in the bottom of the greased baking dish, tearing it into pieces if you have to so that it covers the entire base. Spread three-quarters of the jam over the bread, then put the rest of the bread on top. Basically, you're making a giant jam sandwich.

Whisk together the eggs, caster sugar and vanilla in a large bowl, then slowly add the milk and whisk until well combined. Pour this custard over the bread, then press the bread down into the custard to make sure it's all coated. Bake in the preheated oven for 20 minutes.

Meanwhile, melt the butter and the remaining jam together.

Remove the dish from the oven. Pour the melted butter and jam over the top and sprinkle with the icing sugar. Put it under the grill until the top turns golden.

Let the pudding cool slightly before serving with custard, ice cream or cream (or all three if you're anything like me).

CHESTER CAKE

SERVES 12

As well as being a chef, I also worked in bakeries for many years and this was our go-to zero-waste cake that we made at the end of every week. Also known as gur cake in Dublin or donkey's gudge in Cork, it uses up bits of cake, sponges, scones and tarts – icing and all – that for some unknown reason you never got to eat when they were fresh and at their best. I normally keep uneaten cakes and scones of any type in the freezer until I have enough to make this.

350g leftover scones, banana bread, fruit cake, sponge cake, carrot cake, etc.

225g light brown sugar

75g plain flour

50g butter, softened, plus extra for greasing

1 tsp baking powder

180g sultanas or raisins

1 egg

200ml cold tea

150ml milk

350g shop-bought shortcrust pastry, thawed if frozen

icing sugar, for dusting

Preheat the oven to 200°C (180°C fan). Grease a baking tray (approx. 25cm x 30cm) with some butter and line with non-stick baking paper.

Put all the leftover scones, cakes, etc. in a large mixing bowl. Using an electric mixer, gently mix on a low speed until it all becomes like coarse breadcrumbs. Add the sugar, flour, butter and baking powder and mix until well combined. Add the sultanas or raisins and mix again, then still on a low speed, add the egg, cold tea and milk.

Divide the pastry in half. Roll out one half to fit your tray and put it on the bottom. Spoon in the filling and gently press it down so it's even. Roll out the other half of the pastry and put it on top. Using a fork, prick holes on top of the pastry all over.

Bake in the preheated oven for 50 minutes, until the filling is set and the pastry is golden. Remove from the oven and let the cake cool in the tray, then sprinkle with icing sugar and cut it into squares.

CHOCOLATE TRUFFLES

MAKES 20

The type of truffle you make here really depends on the time of year. It's a great way to use up celebration cakes that can be lying around the kitchen for days at the holidays, when you can't face another bite – think mince pies at Christmas, bracks at Halloween, cakes at Easter. I'm not sure if these are even technically a truffle, but it sounded good and they taste great.

350g leftover cake (fruit cake, mince pies, Christmas pudding, bracks, etc.)

zest and juice of ½ orange

1 shot of Irish cream liqueur or brandy

2 dessertspoons cocoa powder, plus extra for dusting and decorating

1 tsp vanilla extract

½ tsp grated nutmeg

½ tsp ground cinnamon

½ tsp ground ginger

200g chocolate (any kind), chopped

TO DECORATE:

toasted chopped nuts

chocolate sprinkles

Put the cake in a food processer and blend into crumbs, then add everything else except the chocolate and blend until it becomes a paste. Depending on the type of cake, you may need to add some water or a little more Irish cream or brandy. You should be able to form the mix into balls, but it should not be too sticky.

Sprinkle some cocoa powder on your hands and roll the mix into small bite-sized balls. Put on a plate and put in your fridge for 1 hour to firm up.

In the meantime, melt your chocolate in the microwave in 20-second intervals, stirring each time, or in a bain-marie (a heatproof bowl set over a pan of gently simmering water, making sure the water doesn't touch the bottom of the bowl).

Allow to cool slightly, then roll your truffles in the melted chocolate. Decorate with toasted chopped nuts, chocolate sprinkles or cocoa powder. Refrigerate again for 20 minutes. They are now ready to eat or you can keep them in an airtight container in the fridge.

INDEX

aquafaba 42–43

bananas 12

  banana skin chutney 17

beetroot

  salt-baked beetroot and leaf salad with goat cheese and pickled beet stalks 10–11

bhajis, cauliflower 40–41

bread

  and whey 29

  bread and jam pudding 63

  bread hummus 19

  breadcrumbs 18

  croutons 18

  eggy bread 19

  five ways with stale bread 18–19

  flatbreads 40–41, 55

  garlic bread 19

  ribollita 22

  sourdough panzanella 20

  whey hey hey bread 28

broccoli 12, 23

  broccoli stalk slaw 37

  broccomoli 38

  pesto 37

  roast stalks and dukkah 37

  soup 37

  stir-fry 37

cabbage

  empty-the-fridge kimchi 52–53

  roast cabbage wedges 44–45

cake

  Chester cake 64

  chocolate truffles 65

carrot

  carrot and chilli Scotch eggs 32–33

  carrot skin crisps 24–25

  carrot skin dukkah 6–7

  carrot top pesto 6–7

  roasted carrots 6–7

cauliflower

  cauliflower bhajis with coriander yogurt and flatbreads 40–41

  cauliflower cheese 55

  piccalilli 15

celery

  how to regrow 31

cheese

  beetroot leaf salad with goat cheese 10–11

  cauliflower cheese 55

  cheesy kimchi toastie 56–57

  flatbreads 55

  fritters 24–25

  mac 'n' cheese 54

  Parmesan rinds 54, 60

  quiche 55

  ricotta 26–27

  tarts 55

Chester cake 64

chickpeas

  aquafaba 42–43

  hummus 44–45

chilli

  carrot and chilli Scotch eggs 32–33

  kosho 47, 60

  oil 20, 34, 44–45

chocolate

  chocolate chip and coffee grounds cookies 62

chocolate truffles 65

chutney

  banana skin chutney 17

closed loop recipe 4

coffee

  chocolate chip and coffee grounds cookies 62

cookies

  chocolate chip and coffee grounds cookies 62

coriander

  coriander yogurt 40–41

croutons 18

cultured vinegar 46

dukkah

  carrot skin dukkah 6–7

  roast broccoli stalks with dukkah 37

eggs

  aquafaba substitute for 43

  carrot and chilli Scotch eggs 32–33

  eggy bread 19

  sauerkraut fritters with poached eggs 59

  sourdough panzanella with crispy egg 20

empty-the-fridge kimchi 52–53, 56–57

fermentation

  five ways with 46–50

  top tips 51

flatbreads 40–41, 55

fritters

  cheese 24–25

  sauerkraut 59

garlic bread 19

gnocchi with homemade ricotta 26–27

goat cheese
  beetroot leaf salad with goat
    cheese 10–11
how to regrow food 30–31
hummus 44–45
  bread hummus 19
jam
  bread and jam pudding 63
kefir 48
kimchi 47
  empty-the-fridge kimchi
    52–53, 56–57
kombucha 48
kosho 47, 60
labneh 6–7
lettuce
  how to regrow 30
margarita
  pineapple tepache
    margarita 61
mayonnaise
  aquafaba mayonnaise 43
  Bloody Mary mayo 56–57
meringues 42
milk
  bread and jam pudding 63
  cheese fritters 24–25
  homemade ricotta 26–27
  homemade yogurt 39, 59
  kefir 48
  whey 29
mushrooms
  pasta with mushrooms, kosho
    and toasted Parmesan
    rind 60
noodles
  pumpkin noodles 8–9
  vegetable ramen 34
pak choi

how to regrow 30
panzanella 20
pasta
  with herb pesto, cheese
    fritters and carrot skin
    crisps 24–25
  with mushrooms, kosho and
    toasted Parmesan rind 60
pavlova 42
peanuts
  with roast cabbage wedges
    44–45
pesto
  broccoli pesto 37
  carrot top pesto 6–7
  herb pesto 24–25
piccalilli 15, 32–33
pickles
  piccalilli 15, 32–33
  pickled beet stalks 10–11
  simple veg pickle 14
  whey 29
pineapple
  pineapple tepache margarita
    61
potatoes
  gnocchi with homemade
    ricotta 26–27
  potato hash with broccomoli
    38
pumpkin
  pumpkin noodles with
    roasted pumpkin seeds
    and pumpkin skin lardons
    8–9
ramen
  vegetable ramen 34
ribollita 22
ricotta 26–27

roast cabbage wedges with
  hummus, peanuts and chilli
  oil 44–45
roasted carrots with carrot skin
  dukkah, carrot top pesto and
  labneh 6–7
salt-baked beetroot and leaf
  salad with goat cheese and
  pickled beet stalks 10–11
sauerkraut 50
  sauerkraut fritters with
    poached eggs and
    homemade yogurt 59
simple veg pickle 14
sourdough panzanella with
  crispy egg, chilli dressing
  and pickles 20
spring onions
  how to regrow 30
storage 12–13
tepache 61
toastie
  cheesy kimchi toastie 56–57
truffles
  chocolate truffles 65
UN Chefs' Manifesto 3
vegetable
  and salt seasoning 23
  ramen 34
  stock 23
vinegar
  cultured vinegar 46
whey 27, 29
  bread 28, 29
whipped cream, aquafaba 43
yogurt
  coriander 40–41
  homemade 39, 59
  labneh 6–7

Nine Bean Rows

23 Mountjoy Square

Dublin, D01 E0F8

Ireland

@9beanrowsbooks

ninebeanrowsbooks.com

NINE
BEAN
ROWS

Blasta Books is an imprint of Nine Bean Rows Books Ltd.

@blastabooks blastabooks.com

First published 2023

Copyright © Conor Spacey, 2023

ISBN: 978-1-9993799-7-1

Editor: Kristin Jensen

Series artist: Nicky Hooper
nickyhooper.com

Designer: Jane Matthews
janematthewsdesign.com

Proofreader: Jocelyn Doyle

Printed by L&C Printing Group, Poland

The paper in this book is produced using pulp from managed forests.

About the author

Conor Spacey has worked in the food industry for more than 30 years, but over the last 15 years he's done a deep dive into sustainability and our broken food system to become one of the industry leaders in zero-waste kitchens. Most recently, Conor has worked with the United Nations Sustainable Development Goals to establish the Chefs' Manifesto, a community of over 900 chefs across 100 countries that works with many NGOs to make real change. Conor has received many accolades for his work in sustainability and attends events around the world for pop-ups, talks and demos. You can also catch him on Virgin Media's *Six O'clock Show* showcasing zero-waste meals.

 @spacey_chef